The Uses of Adversitv

4/01

For Michael!
with a dmination
for your work -
Ron

Pitt Poetry Series

ED OCHESTER, EDITOR

THE FUNNIES

He waited for the Sunday funnies every
Saturday night—the newsboy's wagon clattering
down the street outside his house—paying
most of his allowance to get them early.
"Mandrake the Magician," "Li'l Abner,"
the weekly serials structuring his world.
Would Lothar rescue Mandrake from the wizard
who'd enslaved him? Would Daisy Mae recover

from one more disappointing Sadie Hawkins
Day? What danger could there be in Shmoos,
those bowling-pin–shaped creatures who'd refuse
their owners nothing? On Sundays with his sins
in hand, he sat in Sunday school, and dreamed
the world into neat panels, clipped and saved.

THE VOYEUR

I was twelve, my new reflector telescope
on the lawn. I couldn't wait till evening
what with all the things to see: the house up
the street where mysterious young women
did unspeakable sweet things; Mickey Cohn's
woodshed where his father beat him up;
or even just some unsuspecting pedestrian,
far away, preoccupied with his thoughts.

But first I aimed it at the naked sun,
my mind's eye lit by solar flares, sunspots,
coronas, when it occurred to me that,
magnified, it might be too bright to see.
I put some photo negatives over the lens
and watched my wayward eye go up in flames.

WEIRD TALES

H. P. Lovecraft knew the greatest horrors
were those that had no names, and so his stories
about "the thing on the doorstep," "the unnameable,"
or entities that crawled out of the pages
of *The Necronomicon*—Cthulhu,
Yog-Sothoth (named but unpronounceable),
forces lurking just around the corner
of every small boy's dark imagination—

called to me from far-off Arkham House,
Sauk City, Wisconsin, to take the trolley car
downtown (me just thirteen, and this St. Louis)
to all the used and dirty bookstores where
I'd find *Weird Tales* and (more than I bargained for)
wonders, unpronounceable and nameless.

THE TIVOLI

It Came from Outer Space, This Island Earth,
The Blob, The Creature from the Black Lagoon,
would call us every Saturday afternoon,
giddy with expectation, to venture forth
from our safe lawns and houses, tree-lined lanes,
to the run-down, dangerous boulevard of abandoned
bars and store fronts and the matinees
our mothers seemed to think would rot our brains,

a thought we found attractive. Once inside
the threadbare theater, the eerie music prizing
our childish lives away, astride the cock-eyed
seats, we'd meet the faceless girls, the dark disguising
our terror as the world changed on the screen,
our hands *Alive!* Our alien bodies *Rising!*

DOGS (1)

When I was six years old I hit one with
a baseball bat. An accident, of course,
and broke his jaw. They put that dog to sleep,
a euphemism even then I knew
could not excuse me from the lasting wrath
of memory's flagellation. My remorse
could dog me as it would, it wouldn't keep
me from the life sentence that I drew:

For I've been barked at, bitten, nipped, knocked flat,
slobbered over, humped, sprayed, beshat,
by spaniel, terrier, retriever, bull, and Dane.
But through the years what's given me most pain
of all the dogs I've been the victim of
are those whose slow eyes gazed at me, in love.

THE KILLING JAR

September. Butterfly season. He was nine.
He'd caught the Monarch in the field behind
his parents' house and brought it proudly home.
Sealed with cleaning fluid in a Mason jar,
it moved its wings in slow and slower motion
until, orange and black and damp, it moved no more.
He pressed it in the makeshift picture frame
beside his other shiny specimens.

The next day he noticed it moving. Its fragile wings
straining against the glass as if to lift
it and be gone. He thought of the terror of all
small things, his awful power for good or ill.
But he turned away and told no one. He simply left
the room where, forty years later, it's moving still.

1960

The early evening streets were glazed with rain.
We were fifteen and walking through the dark.
An occasional stray car hissed through the park,
and then the silence joined us once again.
Night lights in closed-up shops and houses marked
their narrow territory. A souped-up Chevy parked
streetside stared at us. We stared back.
And then they were out of the car. One attacked

my friend, arms and legs flashing like blades,
napalm, explosions. One stepped aside and eyed me:
Stay calm, he said. The sidewalk glazed with blood.
It ended. They drove off. We walked slowly
home, the future before us. *It was good, wasn't it?*
my friend said. *I gave better than I got.*

GIN LANE

Coffin makers everywhere. Men on gibbets.
Men in barrows. Men in boxes. Men
on their last legs. Men gnawing on a bone,
making monkeys of themselves. Women,
bare-breasted, suckling their drunk infants
cascading over the balustrade. The wages of gin:
the whole damned place engraved and caving in.
My parents painted just this kind of picture

of excess spirits, alcohol addiction.
So when my Uncle Alf arrived each summer,
his big heart and his suitcase full of booze,
his jokes and bottles neatly set in rows,
I left my parents to their gloomy kvetching
and loved him as I would a Hogarth etching.

STATUTES OF LIMITATION

for C. L. L., 1946–1992

How we believed that there were really laws
against such things. Parking in the dark
parking lot of Community School, our clothes
cohabiting on the floor, the moon's work
cut out for it: to turn our awkward grope
and fumble to romance and love, and make
the whole scene shine, in memory, with hope
and satisfaction. Oh, why did we take

the trooper's word that what we did was wrong
and slink off home embarrassed and estranged
and lose the simple *we* in love's sweet song,
and see the *harm* in harmony. Time's rearranged
us. I am here, and you are gone. Because,
because. Oh, there are laws. And there are laws.

DELAYED REACTION

Potassium permanganate and glycerine
in rose water are, by themselves, inert,
a lovely purple crystal and a soothing
body oil. But take a bottle, insert
ingredients, and mix, secure the top,
and thirty seconds later the stopped-up
chemicals, grown furious and familiar, will
explode. Thirteen and invulnerable, we'd thrill

at such combustion, embrace whatever burst,
shattered, smashed, went up in flames.
We loved all conflagration. The most
incendiary dreams fired our bright imaginations.
Love, where are the bottles, flasks, containers,
for all the burning things we can't contain?

TEMPS PERDU

Sometimes just the feel of an oily coin;
the glint of a fractured piece of mica schist;
the smell of fish in the morning, as the mist,
a cloud of spawn, flips its fin and is gone;
a piece of Bit-O-Honey on the.tongue;
the squeak of a wheelchair wheeling my father's voice
down the long corridors of memory; will suffice
to carry me, momentarily, halfway home.

Proust knew something about this kind of remembrance:
the sweet sense that nothing's irrevocably lost,
that the sorrow and joy of even the distant past
are locked up safe in the solitary cells of the senses
where the slightest word or phrase will set them free
to plunder the land of longing and elegy.

MILK TOAST

And on those days when he was feeling worst,
fever spreading out its leafy foliage,
nausea like a dark exotic animal
in his stomach, his mother offered milk toast
like a spell to ward off evil, and the rage
of illness dissipated. What subliminal
messages were delivered there? Cinnamon
sugar, sweet and gritty on the teeth, warm

milk, and then the softened toast that filled
his mouth with love. A half-century later,
the millennium at hand, no matter how
the world's ills try to undo him, the center
holds. The sweet smell of cinnamon, boiled
milk, warm toast, can save him, even now.

PART 2

The Uses of Adversity

UNTO YOU A SON

I pulled my squeaky donkey down the aisle,
not a job I wanted. I'd been conned
into the role as, helpless, I had donned
my brown terry cloth robe, fake beard and smile,
my dish towel headdress and my flip-flop sandals,
and then proceeded past the pews of fond
old ladies craning to see me and the round
yon Virgin struggling with our donkey's wheels

toward the manger in the chancel where
we knew the plastic would-be Jesus lay
as real as make-believe could ever be.
My father, star-struck wise man, in his wheelchair
urged me on as if I held the key
to Love and his miraculous recovery.

1958

———

I thought I'd grow my hair like Elvis Presley—
sideburns, ducktail, a spit curl in front.
My white bucks, my black slacks, my paisley
shirt. My father said *why did I want*
to look like a pimp, a goddamn pinko Commie?
He waved at me with his crutch. What could I do?
Staggering on his bad legs, how could he blame me
for trying to be different from him? When he wanted to

punish me for something or other I'd done
(like comb my hair wrong), he'd summon me to him
and his thick hand, and, though I could easily outrun
him, I'd present myself, bend over, and, grim
and obedient, take his rage. What could I do?
Sing *Father, love me tender, love me true?*

THE FRIDAY NIGHT FIGHTS

Every Friday night we watched the fights.
Me, ten years old and stretched out on the couch;
my father, in his wheelchair, looking on
as Rocky Marciano, Sonny Liston, Floyd Patterson
fought and won the battles we could not.
Him, twenty-nine, and beat up with disease;
me, counting God among my enemies
for what he'd done to us. We never touched.

But in between the rounds we'd sing how we'd
Look sharp! Feel sharp! & *Be sharp!* with Gillette
and Howard Cosell, the Bela Lugosi of boxing.
Out in the kitchen, my mother never understood
our need for blood, how this was as close as we'd get
to love—bobbing and weaving, feinting and sparring.

THE USES OF ADVERSITY (1)

As if it were some helpful household item:
a polish or a cleanser that could take
the dullness out of things, give them a shine,
or harden them like something one might bake
in an oven. Did it come neatly packaged
with instructions: *Take one three times daily*,
like a vitamin, a family remedy
passed down for generations? Or arranged

for easy assembly by levels of difficulty?
My father, paralyzed with MS, thought so,
and got from God a free trial-size supply
that seemed to me (but then what did I know?)
defective. I tried to send it back, but he
had bargained for the lifetime warranty.

NEEDLES

My father said he thought I was a baby
for fearing needles, he whose body'd been
invaded by all manner of contraption:
hypodermic, catheter, intravenous tube—he
took them all with matter-of-fact de-
rision. They were nothing. But a son
who, at the very sight of needles, whined
and blubbered like a two-year-old—*that* he

couldn't stomach. And so I said, to spite
him (though I told myself that I was lying),
that *yes*, I *was* a baby; he was right.
And to this day refuse all Novocaine,
a full half-hour of exquisite live pain
better than the needle and the numbing.

THE LAST RESORT

And when my father crawled into the lake,
roving like some monster of the deep,
his wheelchair sitting innocent as a beach
chair at the edge of our attention, *Look!* he'd joke,
It's a miracle! I can walk! And then he'd reach
out for me, and I'd let myself get caught up
in his arms, and he'd heft me on his back
and sputter around like a rudderless motorboat.

Minnesota. Nineteen-fifty-five. I was ten.
Too old to be embarrassed in this way.
And so I kept my eyes on the horizon,
the birch and pine resorts of another day.
And then he crawled back out into his chair.
Years later I could always find him there.

ANOTHER THINK COMING

*If you think **that,** you've got another think
coming,* my father would say as he wheeled
his wheelchair down the corridors of my child-
hood. And so I always had a lot of thinks
en route, in transit, hovering on the brink
of an arrival that finally never came. I held
beliefs like treasured cargo, secret, squirreled
away, so buoyant they could never sink.

Or so I thought. I thought that one day he
might rise and walk. I thought that I'd be wise
beyond his expectations, that one day we
might say we loved each other, that I'd always,
no matter what different tune I was to sing,
think that I had another think coming.

MY FATHER: A LIFE

He said he dipped my mother's hair in an inkwell
as he sat, grinning, behind her desk in school,
and hung out at the local drugstore fountain
where she worked, to watch her blouse slip down
when she bent over to scoop the ice cream out.
He said he once ran off to Chicago, where
her younger brother found him, drunk, and brought
him home. Once when he told me he didn't care

that he'd somehow earned the name of *punk*, I thought
the term must have changed a lot in the eons
since he had been a boy. It didn't square
with the man I knew, limp in his wheelchair,
who must have had a son by immaculate conception,
who never grinned or touched my mother's hair.

THANKSGIVING 1994

Elbows off the table! my father'd shout,
and with a sweep of his large spastic hand
knock my props out and send me to my plate,
surprised, embarrassed, and enraged. It seemed
no matter what I did, I did it wrong.
If I was someone's son, I was no son
of his. For years it was the same old song—
the strongest bond between us was disgust, un-

less disgust was but one face worn by love
under the cover of frustration and
disease. Now, listening to my stepfather give
thanks for all our blessings, God's goodness and
His grace, I'd gladly knock my own clasped hands
off of the festive table. I'd understand.

THE USES OF ADVERSITY (2)

> "Sweet are the uses of adversity"
> — *As You Like It*

Even in the nursing home at fifty-three,
hunched over in his wheelchair, unable to see
who might or might not be coming to visit him,
he'd smile at the floor and give it his cheeriest greeting,
and if no one else came, why, he still had his anticipation
to keep him company. *Suffering makes us strong,*
he said, as his head weighed heavier and heavier on
his chest, his hands abandoned their simple posts,

and his legs, like Jacques, complained and sulked and defected.
He always heard tongues in trees and sermons in stones
that told him he'd one day be whole and reinstated
in the life we busy citizens took for granted.
Sweet? You'd have to have lived with Duke Senior, Orlando,
and Touchstone, my father, in the Forest of Arden to think so.

DOCTOR DEATH

Yesterday, Dr. Kevorkian assisted another
suicide. Paralyzed with MS, my father,
were he alive, would have been appalled.
It was a sin. He was a religious person
and God did not approve of such so-called
mercy killing. We disagreed. What reason
had *he* to live? I knew that I would rather
die than end up helpless like my father.

In the end our inner Kevorkians never arrive.
Forcing the tube down my father's throat to suction
him, ignoring his plaintive, delirious request
to *stop and let him go!*, the grand abstractions
nowhere to be seen, I did my best
to keep him and his suffering alive.

SAFETY FIRST

———————

His wheelchair flying down the side door ramp
each Sunday morning on the way to church,
the catheter sack strapped to his leg, the clutch
disengaged, our crippled protests limp-
ing after his exhilaration. *Whomp!*
He'd hit the sidewalk crack, the chair would lurch
from side to side, and then he'd stop and slump
down back into his illness and we'd march

him to the car like some apprehended
AWOL prisoner. I always feared
that he'd careen into the house, or off
the edge of our great carefulness. But now
the ramp is empty. Another Sunday. Safe.
And what we wouldn't give for danger now.

CROWNED

_____

The way a tongue explores a ragged hole
in a broken tooth, the cracked filling or enamel
tracking the thick flesh, the taste buds full
of lacerations as the blunt organ pulls
a fast one again and again, furtive, apocryphal,
stories of wholeness and health cutting us all
to the quick as the exquisite electric pain calls
the shots and the bloody stumps of words fail

to save us from ourselves, I blunder back
again and again to these memories of him
filling his silver wheelchair like an amalgam,
the heady future he had dreamed of cracked,
for all the good it did us praying to God
to bring it like a tooth back from the dead.

COACHING

Run through it! the cross-country coach said when
the side stitch hit. *Just shake it off!* the baseball
coach enjoined whenever a bad hop took him
by surprise. Pain was simply something all
men lived with, welcomed, even. What was life
without some of it? It would make a man
of him yet. Wait and see. Playing it safe
was for girls and cowards. Running a marathon

required prowess, yes, but just willpower
could be enough to see one through the most
abusive situation. Take his father,
for instance, smacked by multiple sclerosis,
who dragged himself through fifty years, and died.
Run through it! Shake it off! his father cried.

FIELDING

I like to see him out in center field
fifty years ago, at twenty-two,
waiting for that towering fly ball—
August, Williamsburg, a lazy afternoon—
dreaming how he'd one day be a pro
and how he'd have a wide-eyed son to throw
a few fat pitches to. An easy catch.
He drifts back deeper into a small patch

of weeds at the fence and waits. In a second or two
the ball is going to stagger in the air,
the future take him to his knees: wheelchair,
MS, paralysis, grief. But for now
he's camped out under happiness. Life is good.
For at least one second more he owns the world.

PART 3

Swamp

HUNTING

November. All the hills aflame with blaze
orange. Platoons. Battalions of hunters flicker
in the trees. The Department of Natural Resources says
they hope the harvest is high. Deer are a danger
to cars and crops and must be culled. Our neighbor
arrives, face blackened, rifle slung over his
hefty shoulder. *We wouldn't mind,* he tells
us, *if he took a little tour of our*

property. Shots cough from the hillside, tear
the air above us. We can hear the siz-
zle of death in the incendiary after-
noon. *Jesus Christ!* he shouts, hitting the dirt, *who's
shooting at us?* As all around us the trees
burn, and dusk ignites as if in answer.

TONIGHT'S LECTURE: THE EFFECTS OF HEAD WOUNDS ON FOOT SOLDIERS, A CASE STUDY

Government scientists are experimenting with cats
to determine the effects of head wounds on foot soldiers. The cats
are strapped to special tables, their heads in a vise,
and shot with military assault rifles. The effects
are noticeable. Without their heads, the cats become dis-
oriented, have trouble breathing, and no longer function
fully as cats. The government scientists speculate
that head-wounded foot soldiers experience similar discomfort.

The cats are kept in cages for observation.
They lose their appetites and often become depressed,
reflecting posttraumatic stress syndrome as well.
The lecturer stops. The congressmen are incredulous,
shake their collective heads. *War is hell!* They'll
approve the development of better headgear for foot soldiers.

RICH

———

Out in the Gulf a sailboat trails a strobe
light of sun. We sit in the condo watching
a dolphin sew the ocean's invisible seams.
Poolside, coco plum, inkberry, sea grape, sea oats,
vie with the Australian pine, the Brazilian holly,
interlopers in the land of alligator and anhinga.
Tasteful pastels. Walls the color of egrets,
divans the tans of pelicans. Beige and buff.

And if two women at an abortion clinic are murdered,
a Fort Myers prostitute slaughtered and left by the river,
a blizzard up North, and the end of the century coming on,
what traffic could we possibly have with that?
We've earned our time apart, after all, haven't we?
We'll sit by the pool and keep the riffraff out.

ALBERT'S OSPREY

Albert is telling his story about the osprey
that, when two other ospreys dismantled his nest,
removing it stick by stick to a mangrove tree,
stayed atop the platform for the rest
of the mating season, going through the motions
of feeding a family, every day catching
a flounder or a skate and patiently thrashing
it back and forth, an elaborate production

for him and Nan to watch. Now Nan is gone.
But every morning they still take their walks
out past their garden plot, their mangrove swamp,
their orchid house, their egrets and their wood storks,
until the sun's too high and they must home.
And Albert's osprey guards his post, alone.

OSPREY

The osprey sits on its post in the Sound,
just like the sketch in Peterson's *Field Guide,*
atop a fish—a flounder, this time,
both eyes on one side of its flat head
looking upward at its destiny: to fly,
after a fashion, in another form, eventually,
as we all must fly, into cosmic energy
or whatever fishy heaven we can imagine.

But first the osprey sits, patient on its post,
thrashing its catch back and forth
breaking it up into flesh and scales
across the wide water, disturbing the morning's
sweet reasonableness, the beak of darkness
always preceding even the most fortunate fall.

SWAMP

In the wet grass prairie the wood stork rousts
up snakes and frogs. A red-shouldered hawk
looks on from the top of a bald cypress,
waiting for an easy dinner. We talk
about the way the loggers cut the trees
off at the knees, the dredged swamp as good
a habitat for tomatoes as for alligators,
barred owls, otters. Somewhere up ahead

a small child breaks out into a scream
that fills the swamp, the loud intrusion sending
up the hawk and wood stork, scattering
a placid ibis. It's been a feather in
our cap, this place whose name's a synonym
for sluggish thinking, being overcome.

Too much beauty is worse than not enough.
What is pretty and perky one by one,
gathered in a mob becomes a menace.
Take these exotic bananaquits, for instance:
the delicate yellow feathers, a flash of sun,
the airy summer chirping, become a rough
approximation of panic, a raucous chaos
of harpies before a terrible feast, ravenous,

the screeching of brakes before an accident,
a massed cacophony in the manchineel trees
(themselves lovely with destruction). Columbus
and his men stopped here before the rum
trade enslaved the native population,
exotic as gods, these unbearably beautiful white men.

THE BAD SNORKELER

Stands on the anemones as his fins
advance their bad ideas among these animals
that live so slowly their thoughts grow only an inch
or so a year. He cuts them off midsentence
as he spins his clumsy unforgettable tales
of land and air. If he barks his shin on brain coral,
burns his hand on fire coral, ignores the fan
coral waving him off, he's happy. He shouts at us

to follow him in deeper where he knows nothing
by name but the eels and octopi that try
to lie their way out of the corner he's got them in.
He's a wet suit full of damage, a trip mine
of enthusiasm, the goodwill ambassador from a land
so far off nothing translates that he can understand.

SEASICK

Captain Bob is talking about Alaska,
how they moved an entire river to lay the pipeline,
how the spill ruined the fishing in his cove
and he moved here and bought this boat, *The Cinnamon
Bay*, and now we're on our way to Virgin Gorda
to see the baths, an early morning squall
swelling the sea until every heaving wave
has us all seasick and woozy, the smell of diesel

fuel and sunscreen in the Caribbean breeze.
And if we reach the granite and lava grottoes
of our imaginations, coco plum
and sea grape on the beach, will we forget
the trouble we had getting here? Can we stomach it?
Our oily bodies burning in the sun?

METAPHOR AS ILLNESS

He wakes up seasick, sleep's calm given way
to ocean swells, the roll of a distant storm.
He's damp and chilled, as if by the salt spray
slapping the sails, and when the tardy alarm
sounds, he's too far gone to heed it. The body
mutinies—it's every man for himself.
Who'll handle the bilge pumps? Claim the booty?
Steer the helpless ship through the terrible rough

night? Metaphor is too easy. Illness
demands the literal; none of this "under the weather,"
none of this "touch of the flu," none of this
evasion and euphemism. Whole ships are lost,
all hands gone, the cargo and the treasure
lost to tropes—and those with health and leisure.

GOING DEAF

As if he's underwater watching fish
on some Caribbean coral reef,
first the littlest sounds flitter off,
flashing their silver dorsal fins in a rush
of color, and then the larger bolder fish
duck under cover and all he hears is the crush
of jaw on coral, the groupers and grunts of deaf-
ness lodging themselves behind his inner ear.

And he's at sea, unable to swim into
the simplest conversation. He tries to remember
the science of his childhood: anvil, hammer,
stirrup—what must be wrong, what to do.
There's nothing but the giant squid of silence
cloaking him in inky isolation.

TOMATOES

_____

And he's up on the ladder with his maul.
And she leans beneath him holding the stake
hard against her heart to keep it straight
as he lets his good intentions fall.
Early summer. The garden brushed with green.
The sliced soil furrowed to a shine.
Bees humming in the honeyed sky.
Nothing untoward in the scene.

But hidden in his eye a vision grows
like mold, like smut, like borers in the corn
of late midsummer, as if his body knows
some terrible secret it, for years, has borne.
Her head positioned underneath the maul.
The sun, the season, his arm about to fall.

CONSPIRACY THEORY

The day that JFK was shot in Dallas
I was in Ohio, a Republican, almost
eighteen, my father's voice still on my tongue.
He hated JFK, and though I didn't know
why, I thought that I must hate him, too.
And so when Ted Celeste burst in the classroom,
his voice a sorrow brimming with the news,
I leaned back in my seat and said one word:

Good, I said. And all eyes turned on me.
And then class was dismissed. And that one word,
armed and dangerous, went out into the world
as if I'd blessed the future with my scorn
which echoed back across the century
like a lone assassin: *Good, Good, Good.*

GUILTY

The doctor threw me up against the wall
(a most undoctorly thing, I thought, to do).
I told you she was fine, he said. *That's all
there's to it, and all I need to hear from you.*
My daughter, three hours old, in isolation—
too red, I thought, too pale, the telltale mark
of mongoloidism in her eyes and palm—
I guess I had gone just a bit berserk,

but there she was behind the Plexiglas
"for observation," so fragile and alone
I thought it must be just too much to ask
that she be normal after what we'd done:
been innocent and privileged in a world
that had enough despair to go around.

DOGS (2)

_____

October. They're out walking in the cornfield
of a friend's farm. The dry husks crackle
as they pass. The six-year-old daughter's afraid
of a dog they've seen in the distance, inscribing a circle
around them, its barks flapping in the wind like crows.
A warm, bright day. The sun is lighting its fires
in the oak trees. Bees hum home. The father knows
his daughter's fears are groundless, and her tears

annoy him. *The dog won't hurt you,* he says, *it's miles
away and it's a nice dog.* His daughter clings
to his pants and tries to stop crying. Smiles.
The dog moves in like a sudden windstorm, springs
at her, its mouth full of betrayal, full of lies.
She stares up at her father with horrified eyes.

ACCIDENT

Midnight. She's standing in the hallway, sobbing.
She's sorry, she says. She didn't mean to do it.
(Her boyfriend is off in the shadows, keeping quiet.)
They were just having fun. A movie. And then grabbing
a bite to eat, on the run. A rainy night.
The wipers streaking on the windshield, reflections robbing
the scene of its usual clarity. But, no doubt about it,
it was her fault. How could she make it right?

Her father's mad. He's glad nobody was hurt,
but there's a lesson to be learned here and he would impress it
on her. Inattention. Carelessness. Haste. Insert
the appropriate word into her distress. It
was a dangerous world. *That's* what he meant.
His anger swerving toward an accident.

IN OUR PARENTS' BED

Pipe smoke. The faint stale aroma of cherry blend.
The old man smell of . . . what? Sweat? Death?
Or just the dried remains of lather and after-
shave? And then *her* smell—garlic, hair
dye, some vaguely flowery oil, an overwrought
smell, as if the body's pain could communicate
olfactorily. We're in their bed, their sheets,
the cases their bodies made, the rivulets

where they twisted through their unforgiving dreams
or bunched their pillows up to keep their heads
above water through the drifting fitful night.
And what of our own regretful smell and feel?
The sweet perfume of youth in middle age?
One whiff of our mortality: Refusal. Rage.

OLD MAN JOKES

The jokes are even funny when they're painful:
the old man who, when told that he has cancer,
bemoans his cruel fate, but when the doctor
says, *That's not all: you also have Alzheimer's,*
the old man pauses, shrugs his bony shoulders,
and says, *Oh well, at least I don't have cancer!*
and we're undone, beside ourselves with laughter,
although the premise falls just short of shameful.

Your father falls while talking on the phone.
You hear the crash, the terrible disconnection,
and when the antic phone rings once again,
your mother on the other end, joking,
This strenuous activity's just too much for him,
his laughter in the background's like ribs cracking.

ALZHEIMER'S

The conversation seems more like an assault
than a conversation. It races around him like dogs
he can't keep up with, that occasionally halt
to gaze at him threateningly, as he slogs
through the marshy underbrush of his muddled thought.
He wishes the world, that has speeded up, would slow down,
that everyone else didn't seem so quick and smart
while he loped along with his foot in his mouth like a clown

upstaged by the dogs he's trained. His family. His wife.
His friends with their witty scripts, their jibes and one-liners
that, try as he might, he simply can't, for the life
of him, match. His tongue has become one of those old-timers
he used to watch shuffling along the edges of the day,
eternity nipping at their heels, with nothing to say.

AT THE VIETNAMESE RESTAURANT

Her father plops his ice cream on his place mat
and scoops his sticky rice into his lap,
then shoves his fortune cookie at his wife,
insists it's hers. What should her mother do?
Spoon-feed him? Be embarrassed? Or pretend
that nothing's wrong? What happened to the man
she's known for fifty years? Where has he gone?
He checks his watch as if he still can read it.

It's late. It's late. It's much too late, he thinks.
*And here he is lost in this foreign country
with strangers at the table.* His heart sinks.
How will he get home? Where might that be?
He'll smile and do his best to be polite,
although he's seated with the enemy.

LIVING WITH PAIN

Pain, with all its paraphernalia—wince
and groan; grimace, hunch, and stumble—takes
up residence in his spine, will soon convince
its friends—agony, grief, defeat—to make
themselves at home as well, while pain goes
about its business of remodeling its
new domicile: lowering thresholds and tolerances,
removing peace and sleep, throwing fits

about the furnishings, changing doors and locks.
He feels like a landlord with an unruly tenant
banging on the pipes, demanding light
and heat, high on drugs. Pain walks
all over him, won't pay its rent or turn
the volume down. Will shoot, and wrack, and burn.

BLUEBIRDS

for M. W. K. Jr.,
b. April 13, 1977, d. April 13, 1977

We open up the bluebird box to find
a wren has skewered all the bluebird eggs
and left instead its messy unpacked bags
where once soft grasses, song, and feathers twined.
And now the wren is ticking in the trees
like some mad clock that wants to see us gone
as evening, dark and quiet's coming on
and bats begin their homing in the breeze.

We quipped about the empty nest syndrome—
when all your children and their dreams leave home,
their noisy world with all its idle chatter
gone off without your compass or your chart—
and told ourselves it didn't finally matter.
But not this loss. Time skewering the heart.

THE FAITHFUL

He thought about the child addicted to
cocaine at birth, the spasms of withdrawal
that wracked her, and how, when her father, who
doted on her, was shot in the head, a pool
of blood for their bed, she, just two years old,
brought him milk and slept with him and spread
a blanket over him to keep him warm.
He thought about the eighty-year-old woman

who went on with life while caring for her dead
sisters. She thought they were asleep, she told
police when neighbors called about the odor.
And then she wept, and showed them to the door.
He thought about the God who made this world.
The ways He moved. The faithful whom He called.

GOD'S HANDIWORK

We like to vilify our enemies
with metaphor's elaborate construc-
tions. Viruses are hoodlums run amok,
bits of bad news wrapped up in proteins,
submicroscopic hijackers, pirates
of the cell, fierce alien invaders,
and not just the small pieces of inert
genetic material that they really are.

It's easier to think of a devil
conjuring such things up to torment us,
than hold the thought of God in His neutral
corner, watching the proceedings with His
cool, perusing eye, giving it the nod,
looking on His handiwork as good.

PART 4

Mind & Body

THE AMERICAN DREAM

He lived in a country where even a puny mouse
dressed in tuxedo and spats, squeaky clean
and nice (no matter his silly soprano voice
and diminutive size, his arms and legs stick-thin,
his hands each missing a finger) can get his Minnie
(all eyelashes, lipstick, and miniskirts), solve the mystery,
and become a millionaire and live in a theme
park adored by everyone, aging gracefully.

So why was *he* always the shuffling sidekick, Goofy,
rumpled, unkempt, embarrassed, muttering *Gawrsh!*
or the hapless Donald Duck, who, if he
tried to talk—*Wak!*—found himself in a farce
instead of the romance or the thriller he had dreamed
of, while his dog or his smartass nephews stole the scene?

BROKEN SONNET

He always wanted to be one of those guys
who knew how to fix things that were broken,
instead of what he was: one of those guys
who broke things that were fixed. What expertise
could he claim as his own? What small token
of manhood? The tools of the trades were a foreign tongue:
torque, resistance, grain, flow, calibration,
drained him like a faulty valve or coupling.

Which may explain why he became a poet
and not a plumber, mechanic, carpenter, or technician.
But the language warped and buckled when he wrote it.
His best lines never made the right connection.
And nothing ever seemed quite level or true.

MR. NICE GUY

They called him Mr. Nice Guy, and he was.
Always pleasant. Always sensitive
to the slightest needs and wants of others.
In disagreements, if someone had to give,
he did: Mr. Cave-in. Mr. Compromise.
Women found his sweetness, well, *attractive,*
when they needed help or flattery.
Men, who quickly realized that he

would let them walk all over him, did.
He was the rug on which they tracked their best
intentions. The carpet under which they hid
their dust. And he, he felt that he was blessed
to have such friends who loved him as they did,
who gave him grief, and let him finish last.

TO WORRY

Just when he thinks his worries are over, a worry
shows up at his door, shabby, bedraggled, a sorry
excuse for a worry, but then what can he do?
Turn her away when she's come so far just to
see him? She's heard so much about him, how he's
always had time for worries, how his worries
are well-fed and pampered, how he's raised them up
from infants, mere nothings, even the least sup-

portable he's welcomed into his home where they've
prospered and thrived. He thinks that he can save
her; she is, after all, just a small worry, a mere
slip of a thing. Clean her up, give her a square
meal, and she'll grow, be just like one of the family.
He thinks he could love her. He thinks they'll get on famously.

DECISION MAKING

_____

Decisions demand to be made. *Make **me**! Make **me**!*
they cry. But how can he comply when he
sees all sides of them, sees how difficult
they can be, how tough, yet how attractive. No-fault
divorce is what he's after, but in this state
of indecision there is no simple statute
to support him. He feels as if he's married
every one. Bigamist of the possible, he'd

keep his secret harem, make them all.
But, of course, he knows they're incompatible.
And so as he makes one and then the other,
they pack their bags and leave him, disappear
into the arms of underlings and friends
who'll have to learn to live with his decisions.

MIND & BODY

Could he control his body with his mind,
he'd tell his body *cool it!* every time
his body raised his voice a pitch or two
in nervous apprehension, or refused
to stop perspiring when it felt he was
in trouble, or set his hands to shaking by some laws
only it knows. He'd have his body shape
up or ship out, stop being a know-nothing dope.

But his body doesn't care a whit what
his mind is up to. *Pretentious intellect-
ual,* it thinks, as it goes about its business
eating everything in sight, saying *yes*
to whatever guilty pleasure comes along,
the mind the monotone in the body's song.

THE PEN IS MIGHTIER

The poet thinks his penis is too small.
And so he writes about it. How it drew
hoots, catcalls, and jeers when he, in grade school,
had to shower after gym. How he flew
home on the air currents of embarrassment.
How for forty years he has avoided
the locker room and sauna, health spa and nude
beach, wherever all the well-endowed men went.

He always had his pal, self-deprecation,
at his side, humiliation wrapped around them
like a towel. The medical textbook said erection
was the great equalizer. And so he kept him-
self erect whenever anyone looked
and wrote himself bigger than life in his small book.

THE AESTHETICS OF BEAUTY

How can the private parts, which are so ugly—
the turkey neck, all gristle, bone, and wattle;
the bearded monk, suspicious in its cowl;
the fat-cheeked cyclops with its squinched-shut eye;
the pimpled adolescent twins, puberty
upon them—be so entrancing, beautiful
enough to send that small aesthetic thrill
to every synapse in the happy body

each time the hand or lip or tongue or eye
encounters them in any grateful place?
O'Keeffe saw them in flowers—iris, poppy—
oversize, erotic: "I made them big because
I wanted people to see them"; the fleshy pleasure
thrust into the eye of the beholder.

BREASTS

After several nights watching soft-core
porno in the conference hotel,
that guilty pleasure he'd admit to no one—
Nurse Tales, Keisha's Fantasies, Virtual Sex—
he finds himself seated next to a young mother
on the plane home who leans over quietly to tell
him if he doesn't mind she'll be breast-feeding
her two-month-old son during take off and landing. *Fix*

your eyes on your book, he tells himself, as she slips
up her blouse and sets her son to suck, her aureole
spreading out from his eager, agitated, pinched-up lips
as contentment overtakes him, breasts so beautiful
his imagination suckles on them
whether pacified or aroused to strenuous athleticism.

PANTIES

His wife says women simply don't wear "panties."
"Briefs," she says, or "underwear," or maybe
"underpants," or even, these days, "Jockeys."
But the only "panties" women wear are in men's
imaginations. Her friends agree, though one says
she's seen "panties" in a Victoria's Secret catalogue.
My case is closed, his wife says. *Men like to og-*
le women in language as well as in person.

He'd used the word in a poem about his wife
that subsequently appeared in a review in the local paper
for all her friends to see. Never in her life
had she been so embarrassed. Now everyone would gape or
smirk at her. But he's lost in his fantasies,
parading there before them in his panties.

MASCULINE ENDINGS

When one of his female colleagues makes some mistakes
about rhyme, calling some masculine endings feminine,
he corrects her: *erect* and *eject,* he says, are masculine,
while *happy* and *sappy* are feminine. Everyone fakes
a laugh and the discourse comes to a sudden end.
It's not until later he sees that what he said
might be considered tasteless, might offend
even the most broad-minded woman. *Where was his head?*

he thought. They must think he was a prick,
a typical male, always wanting to stick
himself in where he was not wanted, thinking the sick
joke, the double entendre, the pun, the slick
maneuver, the crude or lewd aside, were cool.
(But then, women were humorless, as a rule.)

MERMAIDS

after a painting by Carl Marr

Are they dead, these ravished women washing
in on the tide? She thinks so. He thinks
not. He thinks they are calling him
like water, or the idea of water. _Come. Drink
us in. Swim in us._ The fin of a hip,
a whitecap's haunch, the seaweed hair, an aureole
of ripple and swell, the lapidary tumble
of sinew and muscle, gemstone, agate, lip,

and tendril. Crest and trough of thigh and abdomen.
Anemone. Jellyfish. A wash of aqua flesh,
stranded. Litter of seawrack and sand. Stormy
cargo. Undertow. Succubus. Seduction. _Hush!
Abuse,_ she says. _His male imagination.
Women you could drown in. Shipwreck. Booty._

IN THE GARDEN

It's just like the Garden of Eden, she said. And it was:
hollyhocks, bergamot, coneflowers, and their clothes
abloom among the flowering zucchini;
the lush corn tasseling on its stiff stalks;
her underwear like fleshy shreds of peonies;
him standing amazed in his socks.
And they knew only what the wind knows,
a hummingbird delivering the giddy news

of nectar and plenty and ecstatic generation.
What more did they need to know of heaven?:
Love thrusting them up, one with the cosmos.
And then the coiled sun turned red and citrus.
Bugs and boredom took their bodies for a host.
And they were back to normal. Or almost.

ON TIME

He knows, for her, ten minutes late is early.
She knows, for him, ten minutes early is late.
And so they live their lives together, but
in different time frames. He thinks that she will surely
miss the boat that he's the first on. And surely,
she thinks, when he arrives he'll wait and wait.
She will put herself in the hands of fate;
he'll take his fate in his hands and hold it securely.

"The early bird may get the worm," she says,
"but who wants worms?" "*Late* is just," he says,
"a synonym for *dead*." And so the worm
of discord continues turning surely between them.
He wonders if there's time to save the day.
She thinks that it is just too soon to say.

HOSTAGE

Pain sends a message to her brain:
*Don't move! I've got you covered! Give me all
your valuables.* She gives him her keys and wall-
et. He says: *I guess I didn't make myself plain.
This isn't enough. I want everything.*
She gives him her dog, her husband, and her children.
He says: *What do you take me for?* She gives him
her happiest hours, her hopes, her peace of mind.

Come on, he says. *Give me more!* She gives him her life.
You must be joking, he says. *It's not enough.*
She gives him the world, the universe. He's getting
antsy, his finger quivering on the trigger.
But she's almost beginning to like him. She's forgetting
who she was. She's in love. Her pain grows bigger.

THE STUDENT THEME

The adjectives all ganged up on the nouns,
insistent, loud, demanding, inexact,
their Latinate constructions flashing. The pronouns
lost their referents: they were dangling, lacked
the stamina to follow the prepositions' lead
in, on, into, to, toward, for, or from.
They were beset by passive voices and dead
metaphors, conjunctions shouting *But!* or *And!*

The active verbs were all routinely modified
by adverbs, that endlessly and colorlessly ran
into trouble with the participles sitting
on the margins knitting their brows like gerunds
(dangling was their problem, too). The author
was nowhere to be seen; was off somewhere.

THE BAD SONNET

It stayed up late, refused to go to bed,
and when it did it sang loud songs instead
of sleeping, disturbing its siblings—couplets, quatrains
in their small rooms, began caterwauling—
and soon the whole neighborhood was awake.
Sometimes it got in petty trouble with the law,
shoplifting any little thing it saw
that caught its fancy: happiness and heartache

slipped neatly in its pocket. It joined a gang
that forged currency, bombed conventions, and finally
tried to bump off all its competition.
Through a sequence of events, luckily
it was caught, handcuffed, and taken off to jail
where it would not keep quiet in its cell.

L = A = N = G = U = A = G = E

The poet says that language is an absence,
and a *beautiful* absence, at that. Representation
is an illusion not worth pursuing, a limitation
on the imagination's plate. It makes no sense
to her, she says, mimesis and narration
are out of the question, boring, passé, old-fashioned.
She feels a rancor for the empirical. Abstraction,
disjunction, juxtaposition, and all the other *shuns*

take her fancy. And all the friendly stories
of my childhood pack up and walk out the door,
taking with them their pungent oranges, melons, raspberries,
the sweet fruit salad of the juicy familiar,
leaving us with a mouthful of semiotics,
poststructuralism doing its after-dinner tricks.

LES POÈTES CÉLÈBRES

I, too, know something about the languid
aestheticism of Paris, the Louvre, the Champs Élysées,
and I can drop the right names—Rimbaud, Mallarmé,
Celan, as good as the next guy. If I said
Tranströmer, Rilke, Wittgenstein, Nietzsche, would
you nod your privileged head and languish with me
in the salon with M, or B, and Valéry
in language as insubstantial as a cloud?

I've been there, spent those sultry nights in Rome
some poets dream on, pretending to be cosmopolitan
with the best of them. But give me Cleveland,
Pittsburgh, Milwaukee, Chicago, and a few good words
like *balderdash, hogwash, flabbergast, hornswoggle, con.*
I'll sing with Whitman of *lickspittle, duds,* and *turds.*

THE MCPOEM

I must confess that I, too, like it:
the poem that's fried up flat and fast with condiments
on a sesame seed bun. Steamy, grease-spattered,
and juicy, fluent with salt, piping hot
from the grill, glazed with bubbling oil.
A poem you can count on always to be
the same—small, domestic, fun for the whole
family. Economical. American. Free

of culinary pretension. I used to have to ride
ten miles or so out to the suburbs to find
one back in 1956 when poems were
more expensive, reserved for connoisseurs.
Now everyone is welcome to the griddle.
(I also like toads, and all this fiddle.)

AMERICAN SONNET

Of course, you might protest the Grand Canyon,
the Grand Tetons, the Grande Burlesque (Evelyn
West and her $50,000 Treasure Chest—
as insured by Lloyd's of London) would be
too much for such a room. The Mississippi,
the Missouri, the Snake, would take it clean away,
the smallest windstorm break it up. At best
it might house an immigrant or two,

British or Italian, perhaps. But what's
that in the distance? Emily Dickinson
on her horse. Cummings, Pound. And Eliot's
here, Stevens, Frost, even that grand old man,
Walt Whitman, passing through, once briefly stopped
to trim his beard, have his grasses cropped.

SONNET TO MY SOCKS

If Neruda can write an ode to his socks, why can't I?
My socks are as good as the next guy's—the nylon and wool
socks, the 100 percent cotton socks, the half-calf and crew
socks, the dress socks, the court socks, the tubes. My life is full
of socks—Gold Toe, Wigwam, and Arrow, my New Zealand fleece
hiking socks, my matched and my unmatched socks—you could
write my biography with socks—the black and pretentious
socks, casual and sport socks, the bad socks and good

socks, the stragglers, the see-through, the holey, the frayed,
the socks that have lost their mates, the odd socks, the sweat socks,
the socks that have worn out their welcome, the socks that have played
fast and loose with their purpose, socks with their ribs showing, socks
stretched to their limits, one-size-fits-all socks, socks
in translation, borrowed socks, stolen socks, Neruda's socks.

SEA CHANGES

And then there is the sea and its odd stories
to keep us occupied. Think of the wrass—
the "super male" with his harem, and when he dies
the largest female becomes a male and rules
the fishy roost. Or consider the homely grouper,
how it, to match its surroundings, changes gender
or color. Or take the peculiar porcupine puffer-
fish, how its poison adds risk and flavor

to the feast. And if we caught the fish that grants
three wishes (after the obligatory fortune and fame),
who wouldn't wish for the chance to experience difference,
to swim the coral reefs of danger and change,
to impregnate oneself with the slippery spawn of wonder
and range among the fancy's sunken plunder?

PART 5

Dark Enough

METEORS
_____

The Perseid meteor shower was last night.
We walked down to the lake and from the piers
sat and watched the clear black sky light
up with what we once had thought were stars
falling from some high ledge up in heaven
and not just rocks we rendezvous occasionally
with in space and make short work of in
our atmosphere where they burn up sensationally.

Memory sometimes orbits us like this:
The past will, sudden, flash across a synapse
and, for one bright second, take us back
to some sector of our universe we'd thought
we'd lost forever, some heat and light we'd caught
then tossed aside like any ordinary rock.

POMEGRANATES

It's not finally just a woman's story—
the grieving mother, the daughter's terrible hunger,
the cruelty of the heartless dark abductor
we've come to generalize as hell. Hades,
Lord of the Underworld, yes, but lonely
living as he did with loss and anger
for companions, where only the dead would linger
long, with other shades their faithless company.

We've all taken our turn as sweet Persephone,
abandoned in a world we didn't order.
And every parent knows what sloe-eyed Demeter
knew of losses out of season, the brute
force of time and fate. But what of Hades?
We'd take our childhoods back. We'd feed them fruit.

MORNING GLORIES

Out there in the rain, counting our morning
glories, listening to a nuthatch beeping
up a tree, Mr. Carpenter, dead these
twenty years, appears to me in a dream,
giddy as always, his bony shoulders shaking
with laughter as if over a joke only he
knows. His back turned, he doesn't see me
leaning toward the window of my small room

to get whatever light I can on this
dark day. New neighbors dug them up last May,
mistakenly ridding us of "weeds." Now they
climb the phone pole—purple messages, stars—
while goofy nuthatches tune up their kazoos.
And so the dead rise up with their good news.

COME OUT

Every evening something in the trees
begins its rasping. October. Dusk. Is it
a breeze come up? An errant swarm of bees
lamenting the loss of summer? Or a visit
from a crazy arborist sawing off
a limb on overtime, shredding its dead bark?
A nightingale? The thrush that Robert Frost
heard not calling him into the dark?

As a child I had a favorite toy that, when
it was pulled along the sidewalk on its string,
made just this sort of erratic ratcheting,
so loud my father could not stand it. And then
one day it was gone. So now I'm going out
into the woods to find it. Invited or not.

THE CALLING

He's out behind the farmhouse and he's lost.
Flashlight in hand, the beam true and strong,
he looks up at the stars. The stars seem wrong.
How did he get here? He feels like he's been tossed
up by a storm, a deluge coming on.
The fog, grazing in the pasture, hunkers down.
Which way to go? Out into the darkness
with the crickets scritching their old song?

Or inward into what's been calling him:
the goldenrod, ghostly on the hill;
the yellow corn; the granary and silo growing dim;
the moonless night; the shadow, damp, and chill.
Inside, his wife begins to hum a hymn:
tonight, at least, life gathers him back in.

THE CAT AND THE NIGHT

The cat stays out all night. What does she do?
Hunker against the cold? Sit in her niche
in the cherry tree, black as a bole, and watch
the dogs of darkness circle? Or prowl into
the corners and cracks of a world that we can't know
(inside, asleep, in our cozy artifici-
al comfort), a world of slink and edge and twitch,
of crag and bump and screech and claw and shadow?

When morning comes, the sun, our bright familiar,
preening over a burbling cauldron of birdsong,
repeating the spells that will keep the hag of winter
distracted, preoccupied the whole summer long,
the cat pads home to us on her cold paws,
a ragged mouse of darkness in her jaws.

LIFE OR DEATH

And sometimes, late at night, on a country road,
the moon having cruised over the horizon and parked out of sight,
the stars all wheeling toward their destinations light-
years away, he turns his headlights off, his mood
not suicidal, exactly, but who can say?
The cornfields and alfalfa, that, by day,
do their green business, close up shop; the petty
thieves of darkness take their toll. But he

speeds up, traveling blind now, for a lark.
As if the lack of danger in his life
has flagged him down and now sits shotgun in
the seat beside him. How long will this go on?
His brain and lungs and then his heart jump start.
Life, he thinks, is dangerous. Death is safe.

GOLDEN GATE

Standing on a bridge, a precipice,
he feels compelled to throw something in:
his ring, his keys, his wallet, something he'd miss
considerably. It's a pleasurable sensation,
almost, a pull, a call, a song that gravity
sings, or love. Did Ulysses hear it,
lashed to the mast as his men in their depravity
hurled themselves into the sea? Should he fear it

or give himself up to the wind, the rocks, the sky
in which the atoms that leaped into the void
at the moment of creation still spin, high
on their own commotion, his body's ride
through the cosmos barely begun, the big bang calling
him, his watch, his change, his heart, falling . . .

THIN ICE

What are they thinking of, anyway, those dangerous people
who flirt with the edge of the ice, or drive their vehicles
out onto the lake late in March as if they could walk
on water? Every winter someone falls in, the hawk
of disaster circling around them as the news crew
positions itself around the amazing rescue,
the man who never wanted to be a hero
telling his story against the rotting snow.

Or does the rescuer succumb to the dumb ice, too?
And do the numb survivors ever forget
that faceless man on the surface they never knew
who died that they might live? And does regret,
the thin ice they skate on, ever thaw and let them
through to a summer shore that resembles heaven?

A MIND OF WINTER

The lake is making up its mind today,
stuck with its one idea, refusing to budge
an inch, intransigent, vague and steamy.
Appeals to reason won't move it. It holds a grudge
against the season, turns a cold shoulder,
takes a hard line—the matter is closed—
flashes an icy glance as we grow bolder
and start to walk all over it. We had supposed

that summer would last forever, the lake would lap
at our shores like a good dog, continue to wave
at us, stay flexible, fluid, keep an op-
en mind. But no. There's so little left to save.
Save one old man, waxworms in hand, tipping
the scales, his bright syllables of bluegills flipping.

WAXWORMS

Ten below, the sun on the bright horizon
lighting the ice with a blue, uncertain glow.
The old man, in snowmobile suit and earflaps,
says the reason I'm not catching fish is that
my bait is sluggish and cold. He places his thumb
in his cheek and extracts, like a watery chaw of tobacco,
a passel of waxworms, and, with his forefinger, taps
them apart and hands me what looks pretty much like a maggot.

Here, son, he says (although I'm almost fifty),
and slips the rest of the chaw back into his cheek
and returns to his plastic fish bucket and solitary jigging.
There's something about being out on the ice with a crafty
old man, and the things that come out of his mouth! A week
of Sundays couldn't be more spiritually uplifting.

THE WISH

His friends bring out the cake with fifty candles—
the beer and bar slop fades, the cigarettes
burning their holes into somebody else's future,
the barmaid laughing at all the patrons' bad jokes—
and he's a kid again. A wish dandles
loosely on his lips. The whole place quiets
down as he's thinking of his father—
how for years he wished for *him,* that the hooks

of multiple sclerosis would let him go
so he could walk again. It was a super-
stitious wish designed to placate fate,
something like a prayer answered *no.*
So what the hell, he thinks, today he'll wish for
fame and fortune, and let God take the bait.

SKIN

There's something about the touch of skin on skin—
the handshake, the pat on the back, the arm
around the shoulder, the body's simple terms
of agreement, reassurance, consolation—
that sends an electric buzz to brain and spine,
the blind synapses snapping, full capacity,
to light the body's fires, high on the wine
of camaraderie or love. And if we

find ourselves inhabited by winter,
the mind's blank sky branching nowhere,
snow the best the cold heart can hope for,
buried under time's fraying comforter,
hand on naked back or thigh on thigh
can send us south into the middle of July.

THE SEAHORSE

Sadie finds a seahorse on the beach,
gives it CPR and brings it back
partly desiccated, hardly breathing,
to the condo where it bobs in a jar
alongside her horseshoe crab, her sun-bleached
conch, fan coral, king's crown, nutmeg, whelk,
sponge, starfish, and shark's eye. She sings it soothing
songs as, outside, gulls lament the disappear-

ance of their dinner. She sings Granddaddy how
she saved it, as it dances on its long
extended tail, spouting water, how
at low tide she'll take it back, her song
rousing him from oblivion on the couch
where all day he's been stranded, sleeping, beached.

THE REEF

Another poem has come into the world.
It is a miracle, of sorts, he thinks,
how something that was nothing has unfurled
its feathery cilia, how what was closed winks
open like a bright anemone or grows
over the years like the tiny one-celled animals
that form a colony of showy coral:
elkhorn, brain, fire, until what was

the prose of ordinary experience, the daily round,
flashes with damselfish, yellowtail, parrotfish, filtering
the sun back through the imagination's watery medium.
You can feed them the simplest things—bread, to start
with. Or, for something bigger and darker, a wound
will call a barracuda from the wreck of your heart.

SHARKS' TEETH

Beneath the fishing pier at Venice Beach,
the sun alighting behind him on the water
for the night, he starts to find them, each
slightly different—black, white, silver,
among the mimicry of stones and shell shards,
sea oats and sea grape wavering in the breeze.
He's turning fifty tomorrow. His mother regards
him from the pier, smiling and nodding as if he's

one of the children splashing in the surf,
her silhouette hooked against the sunset. She's
wondering how they got here to this state
of grace and retirement as she draws her scarf
against the evening chill and the great
white shark of darkness opens its jaws.

TROPES

After several weeks in the Caribbean,
when they arrive on the bus at the student union,
2 A.M., the icy wind off the lake hits them like . . .
an icy wind. It won't sustain a metaphor—
nothing in this cold North country is any more
than what it is. The street, the sky, the lake,
the stars reflecting off the lake like . . . stars.
The season comes up short, is in arrears.

But wait! A trope he hadn't banked on comes
shuffling out of the shadows for a handout—
Can he spare some change?—and then it bums
a cigarette, and that small glow of bright
heat fires up a train of thought that takes
him back into his life's *as ifs* and *likes*.

AN ESSAY ON LOVE

Every morning the cat jumps on my chair
wanting love. She sits and paws the air,
a gesture so endearing and so human,
who could deny her? I stroke and stroke her fur
until it crackles and snaps, electric, and then
I shove her out and lock the heavy door.
I wonder what my small attentions mean
to her? Is it merely what it seems:

stimulus and response; act and reward?
Her blind instinctual claim of territory
leaving the mark of her oily scent on me,
taking whatever payment I can afford?
And what about the rest of us? Is it love
that moves and shakes us? We'd like to think it's love.

CAT IN THE SNOW

The cat is sitting outside in the snow,
bunched up like a clump of grass or shrub
in the growing whiteness. Does she know
what she is doing, as our voices, dubbed
in glad cat language, try to call her in
and she stays motionless as the flakes
cowl around her head, as if she's frozen
to the spot for all the difference our love makes?

The night is coming on. The darkness takes
a bow under the pale, uncertain street lamps.
The snow plays out its same white script in silence
as we watch on. The cat just sits and looks
at something in the distance we can't see.
The cat. The snow. The dark. The axle tree.

THE LAST SONNET

Strays into the clearing. Does it know it
is the last one of its kind, an oddit-
y, a freak of sorts that cannot re-
produce, is single, incomplete, its mates
shot long ago, or trapped, dispatched? See
how innocent it looks as it floats
off toward the dodos and passenger pigeons, how it
hums sweetly to itself as some edit-

or sends it back into the past where it
will stay. Night comes on and in the clear-
ing words appear to claim their own: *e'en,*
oft, perforce, and *thither* cock their ear
and *list'* for all the song that might have been.
A pause. And then the world goes on without it.

MAN SLEEPING

He lay awake. He tossed and turned. He could
not get to sleep. The place eluded him
as if it were some far-off destination
he'd lost the map to. If the neighbor's lamp would
just go out, the errant leopard frog
stop his protestations, the garish nightjar
leave off celebrating whatever star
it was that burned its hole in sleep's thick bog.

Minutes passed. Hours. It could have been
years. His father gone. His mother. Even his
daughters passed through sleep. The lamp turned off,
the bird, the star, the bright amphibian.
And then they all were gone, these lights of his.
And he, at last, was left with dark enough.

ACKNOWLEDGMENTS

———————————————

Many thanks to the following magazines and periodicals, where some of the poems in this book have appeared: *The Anglican Theological Review* ("In the Garden"); *Ascent* ("Going Deaf" and "Sea Changes"); *Blue Moon Review* ("Needles" and "On Time"); *Blue Unicorn* ("Hostage"); *Chelsea* ("Man Sleeping" and "Pomegranates"); *Connecticut Review* ("Bluebirds"); *Controlled Burn* ("The Voyeur"); *Crazy Horse* ("Broken Sonnet," "Morning Glories," and "1960"); *Cream City Review* ("The Bad Sonnet" and "Living with Pain"); *The Formalist* ("Delayed Reaction," "Fielding," and "Life or Death"); *Gaia* ("Safety First"); *The Georgetown Review* ("Crowned"); *The Gettysburg Review* ("The Bad Snorkeler," "L=A=N=G=U=A=G=E," and "The Student Theme"); *Hellas* ("Temps Perdu"); *Hurakan* ("The Last Sonnet"); *The Iowa Review* ("Tropes"); *The Journal* ("War Games"); *The Laurel Review* ("Gin Lane" and "Mermaids"); *Licking River Review* ("Tonight's Lecture"); *Many Mountains Moving* ("The Faithful" and "The Uses of Adversity"); *The New Criterion* ("Albert's Osprey"); *New Letters* ("The Last Resort" and "The Wish"); *Nimrod* ("My Father: A Life"); *Ohio Poetry Review* ("God's Handiwork" [as "Pathology"]); *Poet Lore* ("At the Vietnamese Restaurant" and "Guilty"); *Poetry* ("The Friday Night Fights"); *Poetry International* ("Dogs [2]"); *Poetry Northwest* ("Masculine Endings" and "The McPoem"); *Prairie Schooner* ("Swamp," "Metaphor as Illness," and "Rich"); *Quarterly West* ("The Aesthetics of Beauty" [as "Aesthetics"]); *Shenandoah* ("Froggy the Gremlin" and "Where Are They Now?"); *Southern Review* ("Howdy Doody"); *Sou'wester* ("Alzheimer's," "In Our Parents' Bed," "Old Man Jokes," and "Tomatoes"); *Sparrow* ("To

Worry"); *Talus and Scree* ("Breasts"); *Tampa Review* ("Golden Gate"); *Tar River Poetry* ("Decision Making," "Panties," and "The Pen Is Mightier"); *Visions International* ("American Sonnet"); *Willow Springs* ("The Calling" and "Thin Ice"); *The Yale Review* ("Cat in the Snow" and "Dogs [1]"); Yankee ("Come Out"); *Yarrow* ("Osprey").

I wish to thank the Wisconsin Arts Board (in conjunction with the National Endowment for the Arts), and the Graduate School Research Committee of the University of Wisconsin-Madison for their generous support.

photo by Peg Wallace

Ron Wallace is the author of nine books of poetry and criticism including *Time's Fancy, The Makings of Happiness,* and *God Be with the Clown: Humor in American Poetry,* and the editor of *Vital Signs: Contemporary American Poetry from the University Presses.* He is director of creative writing at the University of Wisconsin, Madison, and poetry editor for the University of Wisconsin Press. He is married and has two daughters, and divides his time between Madison and a forty-acre farm in Bear Valley, Wisconsin.

Library of Congress Cataloging-in-Publication Data

Wallace, Ronald.
    The uses of adversity / Ronald Wallace.
        p.   cm. — (Pitt poetry series)
    ISBN 0-8229-4067-1 (acid-free paper). —
    ISBN 0-8229-5671-3 (pbk. : acid-free paper)
    I. Title.   II. Series.
PS3573.A4314U84   1997
811'.54—dc21   97-33954